CROSSROADS VI

POETRY AND PROSE BY
CENTRAL VIRGINIA TEENS

SPRING 2018

TUPELO PRESS
TEEN WRITING CENTER

The views and opinions expressed in this anthology are solely those of the original authors, and do not reflect policy or position of any associated schools or organizations.

STUDENT EDITORS:

Advisory Editor: Marie Ungar
Co-Editors-in-Chief: Astrid Weisend & Chloe Whaley
Managing Editor: Rachel Beling

Editors-at-large:
Mary Dwyer
Artina Li
Baylina Pu
Phia Davis
Winter Molloy
Laurel Molloy
Ezzy Corbett

Book Design by Max March

© 2018 Tupelo Press Teen Writing Center
All rights reserved.

Published by the Tupelo Press Teen Writing Center.

ISBN 978-0-692-08983-5

Dedication

to Charlottesville, with love

"We don't need bigger cars or fancier clothes. We need self-respect, identity, community, love, variety, beauty, challenge and a purpose in living that is greater than material accumulation."—Donella Meadows

Foreword

Every year our students tell us what they see, what they feel, and who they are. Each year you can pick up our anthology, and see our community reflected in their writing, attend our reading and hear their words fill your ears. Crossroads VI, our sixth teen anthology, celebrates the voices of high school teens in Central Virginia. Our home, in their hands.

Each year we seek to provide greater opportunities for leadership for our teen staff, and each year it's the most rewarding moment, to see them building this anthology, treating the work of their peers with tenderness and respect, learning what it means to make a cohesive manuscript that represents the writing of their day.

Let's look at ourselves through their point of view; past, present, future. You'll read poems and prose about our history and their history, and of their present lives. You might see yourself here, reading the thoughts of the next generation of writers, of our future. Enjoy, and our great thanks for reading along.

MIRABELLA
Prose & Poetry Contest

Sponsored by St. Anne's Belfield,
Albemarle High School Creative Writing Pathways,
and the Tupelo Press Teen Writing Center

High School Prose and Poetry Contest Winners

virginia
Josephine Gawtry
Monticello High School

Rough Dreams
Alice Owen
Charlottesville High School

Amazing art of the creator
Elana West-Smith
Charlottesville High School

The Never Ending Brawl
Luke Scott
St Anne's Belfield

Congress
Lily Casteen
Albemarle High School

Tide
Ryan Doherty
Charlottesville High School

Down a street
Javon Johnson
St Anne's Belfield

Songs of My Life Galaxies
Jennifer Bui
Albemarle High School

Earth and The Sky/ Tierra Y El Cielo
Emily Garcia
The Miller School

Orpheus, Eurydice, and Death
Sophia Colby
The Renaissance School

We Would
Chloe Whaley
Albemarle High School

Untied Parents
Simon Jones
The Miller School

Empty Eyes
Sarah Hale
Charlottesville High School

Ghostly Green Tea
Fentress Lynch
Charlottesville High School

Gone But Never Forgotten
Nicholas Kent
St Anne's Belfield

Fading
Chiara Martelli
Western Albemarle High School

Burnt Bridges
Artina Li
Albemarle High School

Why Should She
Winter Molloy
Piedmont Virginia Community College

Entrance and Exit
Lucius Atherton
St Anne's Belfield

The Photo
Johnson Zhou
St Anne's Belfield

In Between
Phia Davis
Piedmont Virginia Community College

Arab American
Maryam Alwan
Albemarle High School

The quiet Ones
Gabe Yeargan
Charlottesville High School

Tears of a Murderer
Aimee Straka
Albemarle High School

Prelude to Prayer
Marie Ungar
Albemarle High School

Hunger
Baylina Pu
Albemarle High School

theories of inheritance
Rachel Beling
Charlottesville High School

mano po (blessings)
Sarah Mae Dizon
Albemarle High School

Anthem
Astrid Weisend
Albemarle High School

Cville
McKenzie Hall
Albemarle High School

Crossroads VI Writing Contest:
Sponsored by St. Anne's Belfield

Judged by Paul Guest, Associate Professor at the University of Virginia, winner of the Whiting Award, and the Guggenheim Fellowship for Creative Arts, US & Canada

Winner:

virginia
Josephine Gawtry

Finalists:

Congress
Lily Casteen

Prelude to Prayer
Marie Ungar

Orpheus, Eurydice, and Death
Sophia Colby

Hunger
Baylina Pu

Ghostly Green Tea
Fentress Lynch

theories of Inheritance
Rachel Beling

The Photo
Johnson Zhou

mano po (blessings)
Sara Mae Dizon

Cville
McKenzie Hall

Table of Contents

virginia *Josephine Gawtry* 13
Free and Lonesome Heart *Johnny Lindbergh* 15
Rough Dreams *Alice Owen* 16
Amazing art of the creator *Elana West-Smith* 17
Moon Trout *Elizabeth Dameron* 19
The Never Ending Brawl *Luke Scott* 23
Congress *Lily Casteen* 25
Tide *Ryan Doherty* 26
Dark Night Sky *Libby Slaughter* 27
Down a street. *Javon Johnson* 28
Songs of My Life Galaxies *Jennifer Bui* 30
Midnight On A Swing *Eliza Smith* 32
Tierra Y El Cielo / Earth and The Sky *Emily Garcia* 33
Apple Tree *Olivia Jefferson* 34
I Can't Have You *D Lopez-R* 35
Now I Know *Chloe Romberger* 36
Walking Away *Gala Misevich* 37
Silence *Kelsey Payne* 38
A Poem For a Year *Helen Gehle* 39
Please Forgive Me: *Mariam Anwary* 42
Orpheus, Eurydice, and Death *Sophia Colby* 44
We Would *Chloe Whaley* 48
L'appel du Vide *Johanna Hall* 50
Un-tied Parents *Simon Jones* 52
The Box *Jeffery Perkins* 53
My Mother *JaLyn King* 54
Empty Eyes *Sarah Hale* 56
Ghostly Green Tea *Fentress Lynch* 57

Gone But Never Forgotten *Nicholas Kent* 60
Fading *Chiara Martelli* 61
Burnt Bridges *Artina Li* 64
Lost Summers *Mary Dwyer* 65
Remember *William Hass* 67
Let's Be Kids Again *Cesca Grazioli* 69
RE: I'm Sorry *Jesse Case* 71
Why Should She? *Winter Molloy* 74
Life's Grey Area *David Lovett* 75
Entrance and Exit *Lucius Atherton* 76
Alone *Carter Gregg* 77
Leaving Home *Michael Babbott* 78
The Photo *Johnson Zhou* 79
In Between *Phia Davis* 81
18 is < Forever *Claire Longo* 84
Arab American *Maryam Alwan* 86
The Quiet Ones *Gabe Yeargan* 89
people-watching pt. 2 *Mansi Tripathi* 90
War Zone *Emma Schmidt* 94
Tears of a Murderer *Aimee Straka* 95
Prelude to Prayer *Marie Ungar* 97
Hunger *Baylina Pu* 99
theories of inheritance *Rachel Beling* 20
Mano po (blessings) *Sarah Mae Dizon* 102
Anthem *Astrid Weisend* 104
Until We Let Go *Eliza Sansui* 105
CVILLE *McKenzie Hall* 106

virginia

Josephine Gawtry

i have met virginia.
she has sobbed drunk in my lap
at 3:53 AM on a rainy august morning
her tears rolling down my bones,
her trembling mouth cool on my skin.

pronounce she-nan-doah.
it means 'daughter of the stars.'

virginia, your pickup truck broke down
night came, and it reached its
charcoal fingers down your throat
trying to find the coal and the lumber.

virginia, i'll forgive you one day
and you'll never forgive me

virginia. virginia. just try to listen when i say
around the break of evening
when your days turn golden and elderly
and become fossilized, hidden inside
a past we don't want to remember

they never grew old.
they only grew tall,
like the oaks.

the child of dirt and water
cigarettes (but not the good ones)

how unfair is it to have no say
in the type of god that bleeds you dry.

Free and Lonesome Heart

Johnny Lindbergh

Forgotten, worn out with the world,
and bitter as he spoke, he took off
after about twenty minutes' riding he made a fire, and sat
for awhile looking into the woods.
He cared neither for wine, women, nor money.
The lilies and the waters swept over the island of the definite world
but he knew all a Christian's ecstasy
against the demons prevail.
As though it had begun to drive the clouds like white marble,
his heart wandered lost amid throngs of overcoming thoughts and dreams
his life in the forest had granted serenity to his soul.
It was his greatest treasure.
He knows love through infinite pity, unspeakable trust, unending sympathy;
   and if ignobly through vehement jealousy, sudden hatred, and unappeasable
desire; but unveiled love he never knows.

"Free and Lonesome Heart" is the first piece of poetry accepted by Crossroads VI staff, that as composed by artificial intelligence invented by Johnny Lindbergh.

Rough Dreams
Alice Owen

We'd be in a car of course,
and there'd be blankets and tea the same color as the sunset
and the steam from my mug would be dancing to the music from the radio.
My feet would be on the dash
and my back against the forgiving leather
and your hand on the steering wheel would be beating a tattoo that neither
   of us knew the road would spill out in front of us languidly
and the dotted yellow line wink and blink
and finally meet the blinking, winking, dotted yellow stars.
The maroon haze of car darkness would gradually creep
over our shoulders from the back seat
as navy blue clouds muffled the western peach sky
and obscured the gradients of mountain blues.
The soft breeze would tell stories in the air between us
of fireflies and nightingales
and the bottom of my stomach would feel that peace
which only comes through an open car window.

Amazing art of the creator
A Cento
Elana West-Smith

Dear God,
if you are a season,
let it be the one I passed through to get here.

Don't worry, there's no water.
Only your eyes.
To love another man-is to leave
no one behind.

For how I become both living and dead.
Like a stuffed hippo for holding in bed.

Once,
I fell into a river,
but wouldn't drown.

If limbs are made of splintered oats and hearts of apple blossoms.
This world's for me.

Unable to desperate desire from pain.
Someday I'll find mine.

Her body knew before she knew.
Soon like hesitation,
it would forget to return.

Lovely weed,
flowering body,
indifferent to the anatomy of taste as property.

Why?
You just wonder just now,
how the mind reaches out from grey muteness.

A Cento is "found poetry" created by joining stanzas found in other poems. This Cento uses stanzas from Jennifer Givhan, Li Young Lee, Jeffrey Dahmer, Avra, Death Mask, Chassis, and Ruth Ellen Kocher

Moon Trout

Elizabeth Dameron

I started by digging a hole
while the birds still slept in their nests,
I crouched, dirt soaking through denim, clearing away dead leaves,
    tearing out weeds,
tearing out tree trunks and then wrenching out the roots,
tearing out pieces of the earth with my hands to make room for something else.
The sun found me shoulder deep in my grave, palms torn
muddying the blue of the sky with the dirt I hurled into the air
shoulder deep, rusty shovel aches at my arms but I am standing in a pool of
    possibility and my heart dances with the anticipation of an appleseed.
I dug this hole, just as I will build this basilica,
I stand in an empty crypt, a wishing well waiting to be flooded
    full of watery wishes, a gaping chasm of going to's.
Shoulder deep in silence, there is nothing but me, the shovel, and the silky
    shadows that slide along the sides of the hole, waiting.

Grey concrete clouds poured out of the sky and into their grave,
    freezing pompeii forever in molten stillness,
    a thunderous silence that seeps into the cracks of the earth.
Fish scales from the back of a trout that wanted to swim around the moon
    sparkle in the cement, hiding in their own shadow, reflecting away bad
    thoughts, noise and nightmares are not allowed in this basilica-to-be,
hold yourself with concrete arms and cement your feet to the floor,
Pompeii is locked, the keys incinerated by human sin
making us immortal.
The skeleton stands like a washed up whale, wall-less and wooden.

Photons float in the empty between, flocking to and fro as they bounce of the
    bare beams, my bones are made of beads, breath rattling a-rhythmically as
    they slow dance to the sound of nothing at all. Frankenstein has sucked the
    sap from towering trees that used to stand in these silent places
waiting to hold the out things up and the in things down, they stand
    like teeth broken upon the headstone for the grave of the moon trout,
    withered wood
waiting to one day splinter and decay,
waiting to be outlasted by their own shoes.
Frankenstein and his monster are not so different after all.

Lining them up, brick by brick, row by row.
Red clay on the skin around my wrists where my sleeves
    didn't quite meet my gloves.
Grey sky hugging close to the ground.
Pressing at my shoulders, weighing on my elbows.
I pushed up against it brick by brick row by row as the bottoms of walls started
    to be, began to start to be, started to start to cover the wooden frame
    that ripped into the sky like ancient whale bones washed up at midnight.
I tried not to look, the grotesque foundations sharp splinters scraping the
    place where the clouds used to drift before they fell into my hole,
    filling the earth with a frame of empty, filling me with sick warnings,
    filling the air with a threat or a promise.
So I covered them up concentrating brick by brick row by row.
My tears fell in the mortar, filling the walls with the salty nightmares
    of dead trees swallowed in five o'clock grey.
Red blocks, drops of water in a well where all my wishes have drown
    with the flying trout,
where I cover myself in plaster
and stud my stomach with shards of glass
waiting to shatter and shine.

I step through the windows of silent places
on the threshold of day and night
dusk scratches in my throat under a crumbling sky of lapis lazuli, skirts made of mist and broken glass russel at my ankles as I step in silent places.
Night falls on my shoulders sealing the faberge egg, and I am made of beads, woven together and tied tight, afraid to unravel and tapp upon the stone floor like rain.
A horn of bone rings through silent places, it calls me with its crying. My own tears answer in harmony as they fall on the stuck keys of a piano as I hammer the silence back together, as fragile as my beaded body. And my heart longs to sing a dirge for the moon trout as the white horse sang, lamenting at the grave of saint mary magdalene,
I sweep the dusty floors of silent places
as caverns cower beneath grey clouds that fell down long ago
I pray to hermit saints, my sleeves stained red as the pope holds his head in his hands and gazes through dead eyes at the mess I have made of these silent places.
I search for wishes in the floor, sifting through the dust of broken promises and lost beads.
I am drowning in the red ink of silent places
I can not breath for all the ink in my lungs, ink in my eyes,
oil eyes of saints on wood watch me so I crawl into the organ, covering myself with the residue of long forgotten notes caught in the pipes, as a symphony of silence rocks my bones,
and when I slither out onto the floor, my boots track it all through the aisles,
and the fever of forgotten things rushes through the basilica and shaking my hands like electric wire. Nauseous furry leapt from the highest pinacle and crashed straight into the marble floor of the mausoleum, furry leaping from the corners of my eyes as my beating heart pounded at the silence

and my tears dripped into the nave, aspersing onto the alter, affusing onto the apse, each a note ringing as it plummeted and ricocheting off the walls, diluting the ink until finally it ran dark from the edges to reveal a blurry burning sun and with one shuddering breath the panopticon cracked
and light tumbled with a roar through stained glass, scorching a sanctuary steeped in scarlet, stained by the silence that used to be.
And the crimson quire called out a love song as smoke shouted from the pulpit.
A trout woke up and walked across the fiery water of the baptismal before leaping out of a window, so immaculately clean it didn't exist at all.
And the organ bellowed as smoke billowed
as the sun's basilica glowed as though filled with humming fireflies
whose lightning wings oscillated as a supernova exploded
and a violin shrieked, hair from the white horses tale lamenting saint mary magdalene on strings of gut and steal that unravel as beads cascade
to the floor.

Ashes ascending
night found me, sleeves soaked in kerosene as I hummed amazing grace
standing in the hole I made
dancing on the grave of the beast I slayed ashes ascending

The Never Ending Brawl

Luke Scott

The Fours Seasons,
(or four siblings who forever fight for their moment in the sun)
    each of them is gifted
they come every year
never at the same time
and never with the same effect
I can sit at my window and watch them change everything like
    a never ending fight for the world to stay their way.

Spring,
she is the youngest, the warmest, the most innocent
    always fighting her brother Winter
taking away his cold, fluffy, white blanket
she brings smiles, but she also brings discomfort her little friends,
    pollen and bugs
pesky little things that always make me sneeze.

Summer,
she is the miserable one, the hottest, too
all the young boys and girls want to be her friend
blinded they all are, by her endless beams of sun
she gives the boys and girls fake smiles and pulsing bright red skin
    they compromise with ice cream but she melts it away
they just get more though,
she is a lot like Spring but also a lot not.

Fall,
he is the mellow one, you can never tell with him
he can be a lot like Summer or he can be a lot like Winter
    or he can be nothing like either
he does not have many friends,
everything green starts to hide from him when he shows,
    grass hides in the ground and leaf makes a jump for it,
    because they know big brother Winter is on his way.

Winter,
he is the greedy one, when Spring does not have it
he covers everything with his cold white blanket
he covers the sky, blocks out the sun
he kills Springs friends, and he takes away my breath
however, Winter brings everyone together
he takes the warmth, only so that we can come together for Christmas,
    Christmas, his endlessly happy girlfriend.

Spring versus Summer Fall versus Winter
the never ending brawl.

Congress
Lily Casteen

There's a place on the shoreline
where the incoming tide meets its counterpart,
and the sand is worn away;
rockweed drawn to sea with the fall of the moon.

Tide
Ryan Doherty

Watching the tide
consuming the glittering sand
washing away
all the debris
slowly moving
taking it back
like liquid diamond
until it flows
to its crystalline home.

Dark Night Sky

Libby Slaughter

The dark night sky
Shone through the long curtains,
waking the people throughout the house.
The darkness was so strong
that the people pulled their covers over their eyes to block it.
The darkness woke the child who cried,
blinded by the darkness.
The darkness shown onto the ground,
freezing the hardwood.
It was cold,
and black,
and troubled everyone,
just by being there.

Down a street.

Javon Johnson

You're walking down a street.
Confused why people are staring.
Staring as if you were some sort of unbathed animal

You are walking down a street.
The overhead lights are flickering like a they are epileptic
the staring eyes turn into daggers—
a dagger with a sharp enough blade to cut the skin
    but dull enough to maximize the pain.

You're walking down a street.
The ten story buildings ahead are diluted as thick fog begins to roll
    in your direction. A cold chill runs through your body.
Almost as if you have a fever but more intense.
The wet fog makes it hard to breath.

You're walking down a street.
Your skin still crawls with a bumpy texture.
A large shadow approaches you.
But only a shadow—one that is only an outline filled with darkness.
As it surfs its way toward you, warmth fills your body.
The hills on your skin begin to erode, and your skin takes normal form again.

You pick up your pace in panic of this mysterious shadow.

You're running down a street.

You're almost to your destination.
One block away.
The shadows surf becomes a swim.
Not just any swim, a speedy swim like that pothead Phelps.

It gains, as you lose distance.

You're sprinting down a street.
You soon regret eating a large lunch.
The shadow is on your back as warmth and becomes overwhelming heat.
    Fight or flight.

You decide to Fight.

You're standing in a street.
Half a block from your destination.
You're sweating from panic and the shadows odd radiant heat.

The shadow lunges at you.
You're laying in the street
the shadow attacks and consumes you—your last sight
    is the bluish grey sky above.

Songs of My Life Galaxies
Jennifer Bui

   a silver river,
that's what I am,
   a shining stream with flowing tributaries,
     coursing through this emptiness like fate's ethereal thread.
Sitting here
under this sturdy starlit sky,
   recounting the numerous ancients of forgotten pasts
     inscribed in jade,
I can see ochna and peach blossoms persistently bloom
   in memory of the immortal struggles like annual gravestones.

Born from freedom,
   blessed by passion;
a lineage remembered by
   amber and sanguine dyes lighter than scarlet
     war songs humming within my being,
   treasured scars among the bodies of soldiers
     like living obituaries
        and devoted corpses of generals
          dying for liberation,
   the chaotic shouts of guards and worried families
     (and songs of patriotism and sixteenth moons echo),
   the coos and elated tears from mother and father
     (and soft notes of eternal heirlooms),
   and the flushed red of laughter and embraced skin
     (and poetic chords calligraphed from pen to skin).

I am a deluge of stars,
admired and beloved,
a river of blood,
   darker than Vietnam's Red River;
   a stream that gave me my inheritance
     in this fragile vessel.
If the living rust in my veins is
   why I'm breathing in melodies of gold and crimson,
then I suppose it's why they're
     the songs of my life.

Midnight On A Swing

Eliza Smith

Deep, cobalt blue sky, so dark it's almost black,
like a sheet, covering our world in the gentle coolness of the fall.
The moon just a faint sliver overhead.
Tiny pinpricks in the fabric of night let bits of shimmering light through.
The small squeak of the swing is just a spot of harmony in
   the music of the night.
She closes her eyes and pumps her legs until she's high enough,
high enough to be part of the sky.
Her hands reach up to grab onto a twinkling star, her eyes shining with joy,
   her hair whipping around her cheeks as she laughs with delight.
She can touch the stars, she can feel their warmth travel down
   her fingertips and throughout her body, warding off the cold autumn air.
But, as always, she falls back down to earth, the gentle heat fading.
Her bare feet scrape against the rough wood chips below.
The chains that she once wielded with power now restrain her,
   holding her down to the earth.
But, as always, she can push herself for a bit more, try just a bit longer,
   and she'll be up in the sky once again, her head in the clouds,
   the moon in her hands, and the stars in her eyes.

Tierra Y El Cielo

Emily Garcia

Entre la tierra y el cielo
están los pensamientos que nosotros olvidamos
y las risas que soltamos
cada tristeza que has conquistado
y cada momento que pasastes viendo los ojos verdes de tu amante
entre la tierra y el cielo
está la lluvia que se cayó la primera vez que te enamoraste
y la lluvia que hizo tu vestido blanco convertirse clara la noche de la fiesta
    Y esa noche era el mejor noche de tu vida
como me gustaría vivir
entre la tierra y el cielo.

(Originally written in Spanish. English Translation Below)

Earth and The Sky

Between the earth and the sky
there are the thoughts that we forget
and the laughter that we let go
every sadness you have conquered
and every moment you spent looking into your lover's green eyes Between
    the earth and the sky
there is the rain that fell the first time you fell in love
and the rain that made your white dress turn clear the night of the party
    and that night was the best night of your life
how I would like to live
between the earth and the sky.

Apple Tree
Olivia Jefferson

As we lay under the apple tree
I wonder why you look at me,
why you set your gaze on me,
rather than the apples that hang above your head
rather than the branches dressed with leaves that weave in and out of each other
rather than the sky painted with golden oranges and soft pinks
with purples bursting in small spurts
the scene was so beautiful, so breathtaking
as if it was a painting or a figment of my imagination,
so why look at me as we lay under that apple tree
but then I look at you and begin to understand.

I Can't Have You

D Lopez-R

Quiet laughter and foreheads against each others
looking into a somber night filled with music from
   the tapping of our fingers,
a mere thought
and a lonely person
bring back the original feelings.
I'm tired of all this quiet
I want to hear your voice
hear me
hear you
your voice in my ears
making me shake with anticipation
making my heart shake and wonder
swirling in a galaxy of purple
from Red
to Blue
I became Purple,
an Orchid growing between us,
I want you to have it.

Now I Know
Chloe Romberger

The tide goes in and out
like the air from my lungs,
and the ocean eating away the sand
like how he stole my heart,
and broke it
and gave it back
in pieces.
Wheels on the bikes spinning infinitely
like my mind constantly constantly wondering
why I do these things to myself
why I let this happen,
time and time again
he took what was mine
and broke it
he put it back together
and broke it again.
Wasn't worth it
wasn't ever ever worth it,
so now I know.

Walking Away
Gala Misevich

It hurts, in my chest it burns
right above my heart,
I swear it's not just in my head
there is no medicine, no treatment
not for my ailment

and I wish I could forget,
forget you
forget what I felt
I wish I could be numb,
numb to the past we shared
all those memories
they make my heart ache
all I want is for it to go away,
this agony
I wish I could erase you from my mind.

Everything you said to me
all the little things you did
the big things too,
they make me slip a little more
but I know I can't fall back into your arms
if I do I'll be lost,
lost in all that we were
I'll just have turn away,
away from you
away from our past
away from all that I've loved,
I'm turning my back on you now
and all that I thought you were.

Silence

Kelsey Payne

I've gotten used to your voice,
to the sound my phone makes when it's you.
And when all I hear is silence,
it tears my heart in two.

Hello?
Are you still there?
Hello.....
What's going on?

It was deafening,
the silence pouring from my phone.
Not a text.
Not a call.
Not a trace.
That you were even here.
What could have gone wrong?
Where could you be hiding?
Why must you make me suffer?
Through this silence.

A Poem For a Year

Helen Gehle

he runs his fingers over the keys as he sits
waiting for the dust to clear and for the notes to settle
her heartbeat counts him in
1, 2, 3, 4
begin

it starts with a list of wished words
one at a time you remember them
the lines to lost poems
the umbrella you never carry
how many days have passed since the piano was unlocked

if you flipped back a few pages
took away a month and added seconds to the year
you might be able to find it somewhere
it's been a while

then there are the other things to remember:
rebuilding
undoing
how the listing of spells
is the listing of all the things you want to come true
because the wishes aren't working
your eyelashes curl too easy and the clocks hardly line up anymore
and in case you forgot, dandelions don't bloom in the winter

he pauses
the music hasn't left
somehow he holds it in the air
not reverently, but with a coexistence
that you see in everything now

you see it in the dashes and dots that run next to the love letters
you copied by hand onto thin blue lines
written by zelda, for zelda
the '20s were a long time ago
but you still glimpse her parasol wavering through crowds
and you understand her tightrope love

you see it in his fingers stumbling along piano keys
until he gets to the chorus
he knows that part every time
it's almost like it plays itself
and as the pedals of the piano clang at the end of each verse
you keep spinning

and there are the things you have remembered:
things to cross off the list
the checkmarks slant like the glint of the light off a sundial
its triangular shadow marking the time
forcing the minutes to inch on
counting down the calendar

but somehow when the hour ends the music doesn't stop
and you wonder why time has
and the calendar lays there in its series of mathematical errors
the radio turned up one notch too loud
and you go to what was supposed to be the end
write another verse

open the calendar and tack on another box, another day

you number it with infinity, for him

and the piano plays on

Please Forgive Me:
Mariam Anwary

I am sorry for not holding your hand or saying goodbye for the last time
it never occurred to me that we were going to be apart
the hands that held me when I was born would not be able to hold me again
the hands that wiped away tears as we were getting ready to say goodbye
I will not be able to feel that hand and its warmth
I am sorry for not looking into your eyes
those eyes that give anyone hope and a sense of security
I am sorry for not taking the time to say the things I should have said
the things I wanted to say were, "I love you
    and I will never forget your presence."
These words choked me inside while I was determined to not face the
    reality that you will be away from us on the other side of the world.
I can't brush away the fact of not saying "I love You" in person
please for just a second embrace me in your warmth.
I have been dying for that embrace since I last saw you
I am sorry for not spending time with you when I had the chance
we are like streaming water we may flow to different places
    in the end we will intertwine and flow together as one
I am sorry for saying those words that penetrated like a knife
"I don't love you anymore and you don't mean anything to me anymore"
these were meant as a shield to defend myself
I said these words in desperation only when I could not bear
    the separating from you
I can't understand how you've forgotten our relationship
    that was established on never ending
promises of not letting anything break the trust
    that was woven throughout the years it has been

the promise to never let go of each other and to always be
    in each other's hearts and souls
our promise was broken like a shattered glass
broken and shattered when you decided to remove us from your life.
You can always glue those piece together but there will be traces
    left as evidence
evidence that tells the world "Hey, I broke my promise
    and you are not important to me anymore."
My presence is not important since you decided to let go of
    the hand you held from the beginning of my existence.
I am sorry for not being able to just leave everything behind
for not being able to let go of you and your presence.
I am sorry for not being the girl you thought I would be

Orpheus, Eurydice, and Death

Sophia Colby

The first time I found Orpheus, it was the twenty-fifth of March. I would have said the day was unusually hot if I could feel heat—busloads of tourists were sweating and fanning themselves and stopping every two minutes underneath the blooming cherry blossom trees to drink from metal water bottles. None of them noticed that I was about—that the very essence of me completely enveloped the scenic memorial park.

It was a good thing that I wasn't being noticed. When people recognized me, they panicked. That's why Orpheus was so much fun—he saw me every single time but never made a scene.

"Hello," I said.

"Hello, Death," he replied, tearing his gaze from the shiny black wall with the names carved into it that he was kneeling by. "When are you going to leave me alone?"

"Are you scared?"

"Of you? Or just in general?"

"Both."

He stood, wiping the sweat off his forehead. "Everybody's a little scared of death. Everybody's also a little scared of life."

"There's no need to fear me. I don't hurt."

"You kill."

"Lots of things kill. Not me. I just take away."

"Look, I don't mean to be rude, but could you… could you give me a minute alone, please?"

"I have to stay anywhere there's grief—"

"Please," he interrupted. "Only a minute. The smallest bit of solitude, that's all I ask. I need to remember what it was like before you started coming and going all the time."

I considered his request. "Fine. But *only* a minute."

He closed his eyes. Sat in front of the wall. Traced his finger down the names. Let his hand rest against one. Smiled.

There were places I had to be. A minute turned into a year.

The second time I found Orpheus he was in the same place by the wall. I planned to apologize for leaving him alone so long, but Eurydice stood feet away from us both and she was far more friendly, so I went over to her instead.

She smiled, her eyes crinkling at the corners. "How've you been?" she asked.

"I've been well," I smiled back. "How long until we're finally together?"

"I have a while. Don't get carried away."

I still needed her, though, the same way I needed Orpheus' father, the same way I needed everyone and everything who came to me. They made me complete; they were my purpose.

"You see Death, too?" Orpheus asked, not looking at her.

"Ever since I was little," she replied.

"Who was it for?"

"No one," she said, placing a marigold at the bottom of the wall. "I'm... quite ill, that's all."

"Oh, I'm so sorry. I just assumed—with the flower and everything—"

"No, no, don't apologize. I made my peace with it a long time ago. I'm just here because I like to... pay my respects, I guess. These people were incredible. They gave their lives for our country. America isn't perfect by any means, but it's thanks to them that we have the chance to make it better. It's good to remember that sometimes."

He met her eyes. "I'm Orpheus."

"Eurydice."

The third time I found Orpheus, he was with Eurydice in a hospital waiting room. I was in that building more often than not during those days. I missed when people died in their homes. I would look at their possessions—the books in their libraries, the paintings on their walls—and make guesses as to what kind of people they were. I couldn't do that anymore.

"What did they say?" asked Orpheus, grasping Eurydice's hands as I drifted past them.

"Two more years."

"Two?" he repeated.

"If I'm lucky."

"And there's nothing—I mean, they tried *everything*?"

"We have two more years together," she smiled. "And I'm spending every moment of them with you."

"Nothing would make me happier, Eurydice. No one makes me happier than you do."

The time Orpheus found me was just over two years later, in the very same hospital.

"Death," he said. "Why her?"

"I don't know what you mean."

"Why did you kill her?"

I was unsure whether he was angry or sad. Feelings were complicated. "I didn't kill her," I corrected him. "I just took her away."

"Well, bring her back," he demanded.

"I don't work like that. I can't bring people back."

"You can in the stories."

"Stories?"

"You know—Hades, Pluto, Osiris."

"Those are fictional characters, Orpheus. They're the result of humanity's discomfort with its own mortality. They're rationalizations of inevitable biological processes, and nothing more."

"Have you ever loved anyone?"

"What does that *mean*?"

"When someone makes you so happy that you can't imagine existing without them, when you think about them all the time, when they complete you—that's love. You—a rationalization of you loves Persephone in stories."

I understood what he said. I couldn't imagine existing without those who came to me. I thought about them all the time. They completed me. "I can't give Persephone back to you," I said.

"Eurydice," he corrected.

"You said the name of the person I love is Persephone."

"Please," he begged, growing more frustrated and desperate. "I'm sick of talking in circles with you. Just give me my wife."

"She's gone, Orpheus. Be sensible."

"You say you take people away. So just—take me away. Take me to wherever you took

her. We could be together again, in that place."

"Hmm," I contemplated, not quite sure if I wanted him. "This decision is irreversible—"

"Just do it for me—for your *friend*. Show me mercy."

"Wherever you think I'm going to take you, Orpheus—"

"I'm done with this."

"The place you're thinking of might not exist. Nobody knows besides the people who

live there—*if* people live there, which—once again—they might not."

"I don't care. Just take me away. Please. I'm done."

"Are you sure?"

"Completely and entirely." He placed his hand in mine.

"Well then. Persephone, it's nice to meet you," I smiled. But he was already gone.

We Would
Chloe Whaley

We would sit on a hill
and talk about life.
You'd tell me about the '50s
about the ten cent steak dinners
about the fear of selection to serve.

We would look on at the world
and be awed by its beauty.
You'd say that it had diminished,
years ago flowers were gold,
years ago birds were plenty.

We would sit on a hill
and talk about change.
You'd tell me how the world was different
how maybe it was for the best,
how you would go back to the old days.

We would look on at the world
and think of how the sun feels on our faces.
I'd say that our days together were the best
that I wish I had lived in the years long ago
that I could sit here all day long.

We will do this when I die
but for now it'll just be a thought.
Disease has taken you from this world,
taken you, a true hero,
taken you, a man who was loved by all.

We will never understand why God chose you,
and all I know is that you won't be in pain.
You can sit on hills of gold flowers,
sit with birds all around
sit with your ten cent steak dinner.

I will meet you again one day,
and I will say I love you.
Because I didn't that day,
that day,
that day.

You will forgive me
and know that I didn't mean to forget.
You will be waiting for me,
waiting to go sit on a hill and
waiting to talk about life.

We will do as I dreamt the night you died,
and it will be more than before.
I will forget my anger towards you for leaving,
forget my sadness when you left and
remember that God had a plan.

L'appel du Vide

Johanna Hall

This morning I didn't make my bed.
I woke up as tired as when
I lay down
and for some reason
I took it out on the sheets.
And I can't go back and do it over again
because I left the house hours ago
and for some reason that bothers me,
the unfinished act of waking up
haunting my footsteps.

I am nothing but suicide watch hospital visits
the prick of the IV so familiar
to my veins

I am a lighthouse deserted by the sea
and still I watch
night after night
for waves that will never crash
on these shores again

You know that feeling
when something presses against your throat
and the tension leaves you choking?
That's what today is.

Today is hollow.

Did I fall or let go?
I can't remember.
I mean, I do.
At least, I remember remembering.
I remember touching the memory hesitantly
and feeling it crawl out from underneath me
unafraid to go

Maybe my wishes never come true
because I never look at the stars anymore—
at least, never with hope.
Or maybe my eyelashes have held on
my whole life
refusing to float
onto my cheekbones
I wouldn't blame them.

Am I a plane crash
or a fallen star?

Either way,
embers that refuse to light
tug at my fingertips.

Maybe I let go.

Un-tied Parents

Simon Jones

"Sorry to hear that"
I've never understood why people felt bad

It seems like a pretty sweet deal
to me because I get
Two different houses
Two different families
Two different Christmases
Two separate lives

And yet only one Pair of my favorite shoes
They go back and forth
House to house

It's funny
That I don't have a favorite shoe right or left
I don't put one on first
Or tie one before the other

It's funny-
to me because they are
Two different shoes
Two different shapes
Two different feels

Two separate shoes

And yet they are my favorite Pair.

The Box
Jeffery Perkins

He was left out like a cardboard box on the street. Neglected, anxious, and stranded. She didn't come. The girl of his dreams. A tall brunette girl who'd make any man drop over in awe. He thought she could have been "the one." At 19, it was the first girl he ever felt comfortable to talk to, and after months of building confidence, he nervously asked her out to see the new musical. Now, he waited outside with soaked shoes and his raincoat hood deflecting the cold droplets of water. He looked down at his feet and saw his shadow created by the bright theatre lights behind him, and his reflection from the street puddle looked back at him. What could he make of himself? What could he do? At the moment he thought he had the answer, a truck drove through the puddle and splashed it away. He walked back to the box office and returned his tickets, dripping with disappointment.

My Mother
JaLyn King

You have forgotten it all.
You have forgotten your name,
where you lived, who you
loved, why.

I am your daughter,
I sit here day by day repeating myself,
daughter, son, dog.

Trying to bring you back.
You're trapped in the sunken place,
The mind wanders while the world keeps going.

I point to a photograph.
Who is that?
My son, you say.
I point to another, who is that?
My dog, you say.

I look into your eyes.
Who am I?
You go blank, back into the sunken place.
I am your daughter.

I held your hand when times were rough,
I cooked you dinner every night with school work lying on the table,
I guided you down the stairs when you were unstable,
held you while you cried yourself to sleep at night,

took care of you when nobody else could.

She looks at me and I look at her,
Yes, I am your daughter,
you have forgotten it all.

Empty Eyes
Sarah Hale

The water is clear now.
I hadn't noticed the murk.
Before.

The telephone drops.
Empty eyes. He said.
Marbles, spheres, or sapphires
all blank blank blank
when he saw her last.
No doubt.
Only minutes too late.

Paying no mind to the rocks.
The stream hurries down.
Rushing.

The quiet surrounds.
Stillness consuming.
My face pressed tight against the glass.
To be together
but once more.
Here.
Her hands are much too still.

Ghostly Green Tea

Fentress Lynch

"Would you like some more tea?"

He blinked. His eyes focused on the little girl in front of him, pouring an invisible liquid from a pink plastic kettle into little plastic tea cups as if it were tradition. She looked familiar.

"Uh, yes please." He replied. He had no idea where he was, or how he got there, but he didn't dare be rude to the little girl. He gave her a soft smile and picked up the cup when she pushed it to him. He felt a vague sense of deja-vu.

The little girl sipped her imaginary tea and pretended to burn her tongue. "Bleh! Bleh! This tea is toooo hot! How is yours, Sir Acha?"

"Sriracha?"

"Sir Acha. Like you're a knight but named after my dad's favourite sauce. It's very hot just like this tea."

He placed his teacup on the table. "How... How long have I been here?"

"You got here just as the tea was ready. Perfect timing!" The little girl chirped. "I knew you would come, you'd never miss tea!"

The longer he sat there drinking invisible drinks, the more confused he became. He couldn't remember very much before he saw the little girl, who had a face he recognized but he couldn't place where from. He had a vague memory of a bright light and a figure in a pressed white suit shaking his hand, saying, "You're not through yet, she still needs you!" But before that moment--nothing.

From another room, a woman's voice called, "Melody!"

He and the little girl both looked towards the sound of the voice.

Suddenly, he became very nervous. The voice sounded like it belonged to a mother. What would a mother think of him having tea with her daughter? Would she call the police? Would she attack him?

A very tall woman walked into the room. She wore a dainty black dress, and a golden ring on a necklace chain. She was breathtaking. He felt as if he knew her from a dream. "I'll be back late tonight, sweetheart." She said to her daughter. "You'll probably be in bed when I get home. The babysitter will be here in about ten minutes but I have to leave. Don't open the door for anyone. Rosie has a key. Okay?" The woman lifted up her purse and walked over to her daughter.

"Mommy look at who I'm having tea with!" Melody cried expectantly.

He felt himself tense. This was the moment. This was when the situation would surely go to hell.

But the woman looked at the man sitting across the table from her daughter--looked him right in the eye--and didn't see him. She sighed tiredly, forced a smile, said, "Very nice sweetheart", then kissed her daughter on the head and left. He felt a strange sense of deja-vu as she went.

Why hadn't the mother seen him when he was right in front of her? Was he invisible somehow? It seemed that the little girl was the only one that could see him, as if he were her imaginary friend. He wondered if he looked different to her than he did to himself, and how and why he had ended up there.

Little Melody gave a sad sigh. She began to pour more invisible tea. He began to wonder if maybe the little girl could see the tea, too, the same way she could see him but no one else could. He wondered for how long people had made fun of children for having imaginary friends, when they were not imaginary at all.

Melody sniffled.

"Is...everything okay?"

The little girl rubbed her eyes. "Yeah. I just miss having tea with my mom. She's out all the time now, and Rosie who watches me doesn't like tea." Her eyes grew very watery, and her round cheeks turned red.

"Well, good thing I'm here now." He said, giving the little girl a warm smile. "Tea is my *faaavourite* thing to drink! I showed up just in time, it seems."

The little girl brightened up a little. Something shone in her eyes, almost as if she had expected this response from him. "Thank you, Sir Acha. I also have some fancy biscuits for the tea! Would you like some?"

"I would love some!"

The little girl poured another cup of invisible tea, and placed an intangible cookie on the small dish in front of him. They clinked their plastic cups together, raised their pinky fingers, and sipped their drink. It was the perfect temperature now.

He smiled softly to himself as little Melody began to tell him a story about tea parties with other kids, and how they were never as much fun, and how her friend Meredith always eats too many biscuits, and so on and so forth. He felt as if he recognized some of the names she mentioned. A few minutes later Rosie came in to babysit, immediately going into the next room to watch the television after barely saying "Hey, Mels" and glancing at the table. The babysitter hadn't seen him either.

It was strange to know, now for certain, that he was in fact invisible. Invisible and imaginary to everybody except his new ward, Melody. Was she the one that had brought him back to life? Was it because of her that he had not gone into a bright light, but had gone where he was needed? He wasn't sure. And he wasn't sure how long he would be there. There was no way to know. He had a feeling he would never again see the figure in white that had greeted him and sent him to this very familiar house, and so would have no way of getting any answers. But he wasn't bothered. He was content being an imaginary friend for a lonely child that needed him.

"More tea, Sir Acha?" Melody chirped.

"Do you have any sugar?"

"Of course!"

"Then I would love more tea, my little Melody."

Gone But Never Forgotten
Nicholas Kent

Comfortable, lightweight, sweat-resistant, sporty, matching, beautiful: These are all words that I would use to describe my white Nike shirt, which was worn out way too soon.

Bought at Kohls, some might say not as good quality as a shirt from a real Nike store, but I beg to differ.

My shirt saw many things during its long lifetime. From workouts, to baseball and baseball games, to family dinners, this shirt had been through it all.

But then the tragic day came where my precious shirt had been taken.

After many baseball games in the hot midsummer days, my shirt became stained and tattered at the top. My heart felt a sharp rush of pain for something lost; like love.

I tried to continue wearing my shirt, but my mom looked askance...
"That shirt is stained. And it's falling apart."

"But Mom!"
"Please. Do NOT wear that again."

Now I occasionally wear it to sleep in at night, when everything else is dirty. It deserves more than this. Something better.

And that's why I am putting it to rest now. It was a good shirt. It made me feel like I had a purpose. Like I had something to live for. It was a part of me.

Gone now, yes. But its legacy will live on forever.

Fading
Chiara Martelli

In the grey and feeble light coming through the gauze curtains, the room looks dull and lifeless. There are no lights on, no sounds. The silence is utter and dense, isolating.

She's sitting on the floor, her naked legs crossed on the soft carpet as her clumsy fingers play with a loose thread. Scattered around her, at least a dozen pens. She doesn't know how long she has been staring at the nearest wall; it could have been mere minutes, or hours, perhaps days. She doesn't remember the light in the room changing.

The truth is: she doesn't remember anything at all.

She can't recall the name of the wallpaper color, but what is a name? Does she even have one? And who are the people in the frames, all those strangers with happy faces? They stare all the time, laughing at her, judging her very movements.

Her hands fly to her head, fingers pressing on her skull, hoping it will help her remember something. A feeling, a name, anything she can cling to before falling forever in the soothing darkness that has been tempting her for too long, taking away parts of her. However, no matter how hard she tries, her mind remains silent, a well too deep to reach the memories laying on the bottom.

She looks down at herself and abruptly drops her hands, and starts tracing the dark swirls marking her white skin with her fingers.

A child runs, smiles. The grass is green and the sky
Mama come!

As she reads, the words take shape in her mind, creating a picture, bringing a memory back to her, even though she doesn't remember it happening, or who the child is and what he really looks like. She closes her eyes as she tries to hold on to it, but the words escape from her grasp, swift as air, leaving her with nothing.

Deep down, inside her head, voices call to each other, echoing those memories long gone, but they are too far for her to reach.

Then, sudden and unexpected, an image flashes in the back of her mind, bringing along sounds, smells, colors, faces.

She opens her eyes and reaches for the nearest pen before it's too late. Dark ink stains her forearm as she presses the tip of the pen on her skin.

A hall stuffed with people, laughter and voices blending together with Christmas music. A handsome man is looking at her, smirking, a goblet filled with sparkling white wine in his hand. He laughs at something she must have just said and passes a hand through his hair.

In her head, she knows everything that is happening in the scene, but, at the same time, she can't write it all down. The words get stuck, refusing to come out, still the pen dances on her skin.

Then, with a flicker, the picture vanishes away, and she's left with a bunch of words on her skin that are not enough to bring the memory back.

She throws the pen against the wall with all the force she has left, and her scream of frustration fills the silent room. As her hoarse voice cracks, the sound soon dies in her mouth. When was the last time she spoke?

She gets back to staring the wall, her breath ragged, until the creak of the door opening interrupts the silence. Slowly, she turns her head to find two figures hesitating at the threshold. The man is tall and dark-haired, dark circles surround his eyes and his face looks drained, but it might be the light in the room. The boy is young, tiny, his gaze darts to the broken pen near the wall, then settles on her, scanning.

She doesn't know who they are.

"Why does she do that?" the child asks with a feeble voice. "Why doesn't she use paper?"

"I don't know, honey, I don't know."

She drops her gaze and concentrates again on the memories written on her skin. Footsteps approach, the sound muffled by the carpet, then two strong hands grasp her under her armpits and gently lift her to her feet. She lets the man support and guide her out of the room into a bright hallway, the child silently following a step behind.

Where are they taking her?

They enter another room, and the man sets her on a stool and starts removing the few garments she is wearing. It's hot in there, and the steaming water from the bathtub emanates a sweet perfume. She has smelled that before, but cannot remember what it is.

"It's lavender." the child explains as if reading her mind.

The man lifts her and eases her down in the bathtub, the water closing around her fragile body.

"Can you pass me the soap?" he asks the little boy while she plays with the swirls on the surface of the water.

They clean her back and shoulders, then move to her arms. The sponge rubs on her forearms, insisting on the areas marked by the ink. That's when she understands what is happening.

They are trying to make her forget, to take away from her all she has left.

No.

She starts shivering, even though the water is hot, her teeth clattering against each other. Why are they doing this to her?

"We're trying to help you, Mama."

It's not true, but she doesn't have the words to say that and no strength to stop what's going on. The only thing she can do is watch the ink leave her skin, the words dissolving into the water. Precious fragments of memories gone forever.

What if she will never remember anything again?

Her eyes cloud and a heartbeat later a burning tear slides down her cheek and drops in the water, right in the middle of a stain of ink.

Burnt Bridges
Artina Li

Burnt bridges

  are hard to rebuild,

  not because of the chasm between,
    ironically the same distance,
      but that the ashes make the banks just so very slippery.

Perhaps
  this was for the best,
that
  the bridge was burnt instead of our cities,
    our golden cathedrals, treasured groves

intact from each other's hindering.

Let us instead of bridges,

  fill the gap between us with a century's worth of tears,

and erect walls, miles high,
   o we'll keep to our own wild ways,

      your arrogance not trespassing mine.

Lost Summers
Mary Dwyer

I miss the sun.

The sticky sweet popsicles
melting before your eyes,
rivers of cherry red
trickling down your fingers.

Brutal heat that left
you destitute and depleted.
The muggy, thick air
seeping into your skin.

The bitter smell of dirt
bringing brilliant storms that lit the sky
and kept me watching
for hours on end.

Days that dissolved into nights
the explosion of fireworks
bluer blues
greener greens
birds, everywhere.

I miss it all.

I don't know if I'll ever escape
the sickeningly sterile smell of these halls.
The four white walls
that close in on me more each day.
Beeping machines, bed pans,
and sandpaper hospital gowns.

I would give anything
for just one more melting popsicle,
one more fireworks show,
one more blue sky.

Remember
William Hass

As a baby, I remember you holding me in your arms
Me looking at my reflection in your glasses
I knew you would always be there for me.
I remember Christmases, we would pick you up at the airport.
Mom and I patiently waiting.
I would see you and sprint towards you, jumping into your arms.
You would comment on how big I had gotten.
You would remember how little I used to be.
As the years went on, I remembered everything,
But you began to forget.
Your watery eyes, white hair, and love of Sudoku.
You started to forget.
I remember Hilton Head
I remember having to repeat myself over and over again
I was not bothered, I loved to talk to you.
I remember hearing your same story time and time again.
I remember yelling at you.
"I know Nana, this is the 8th time today you've told us."
I started to cry .
I remember your eyes looking at me with confusion and sadness.
I remember the pain that I felt.
I remember visiting you four years ago.
You knew who I was
You said, "I remember taking care of you when you were a baby"
I felt hope. Maybe you were not as bad as they said.
I remember calling you last year.
The grandson that longed to see his grandma again.
I remember saying, "Hi Nana."

You remembered me as John, you high school boyfriend
Shocked, I handed the phone to my mom.
Broken, I went to my room.
I remember knowing I had lost you.
Today, I remember all the memories with you, Nana.
You remember none.
You remember whatever Alzheimer's wants you to remember.
   Alzheimers did not want me in those memories.

Let's Be Kids Again
Cesca Grazioli

Let's be kids again,
just for a Moment.
Let's find a field of daisies
and stain our thumbs green
weaving their delicate stems through our
mud-brown hair.
We'll crown ourselves master musicians
and the flowers will sway to the rhythm we pluck
on blades of grass.
When the blossoms slow their dance,
their sleepy eyes slipping shut,
tuck them under the wind,
and we'll lie in our kingdom,
letting the afternoon light freckle our noses.
When the sun starts to sink,
take my hand and we'll splash after it.
And maybe, your foot will catch on a golden ray,
thin as twine,
and you'll fall,
tumbling head first
into the Realm of the Moon,
where Her twinkling subjects will flit about;
seamsters of her evening Gown
that veils the sky.
We'll land in a pine tree forest,
choose the tree with peppermint bark,
and find a foothold,
our weathered hands grasping licorice twigs.

When we're perched high up,
our cheeks glowing like embers,
clouds falling from our mouths,
we can whisper secrets into a jar
and let fireflies float back out
like smoke.
Let's chase them on tiptoes,
leaving a trail of giggles
as we pirouette through the branches,
waltzing with our moonlit shadows.
I'll spin into you;
each quick breath
releasing a butterfly from my belly
until a kaleidoscope of silvery wings surrounds us
like the echoes of stars.
They'll warm the air,
blowing our hair into lion's manes,
pushing us until we're forehead to forehead,
mind to mind.
And amidst this chaos of drowsy daisies, sinking suns,
peppermint pines, forgotten fireflies,
and dances in the dark,
I'll press one hand to your chest
and wind a quivering thread of your heartbeat
around my crossed fingers,
Hoping
the new sun will linger under the horizon,
and wait just a Moment more
to bring tomorrow.

RE: I'm Sorry
Jesse Case

We were eight years old when you proposed. You kneeled in the red dirt that was still mud after last night's rain and held out a ring you'd stolen from your mom's jewelry box. It looked old and expensive and way too big for my fingers but you'd said it reminded you of me because of my blue eyes. I pulled you up off the ground and we wiped the dirt off your knees. I held the ring in a tight fist and wanted to put it on, but mumbled about having to ask my mom first. I remember smelling fresh cut grass as we trotted back to the porch. When we approached her, holding hands, she laughed a belly laugh. Not because we were eight years old, but because a girl can't propose to a boy. We didn't talk for the rest of the summer.

We were 11 years old when you told everyone in our class that we were dating, and we weren't. You told everyone we were gonna grow up and get married, and we weren't. You bought us two tickets to the dance and told everyone that I knew how to slow dance, and I really, really didn't. My guidance counselor laughed when I asked her for advice, and told me to just go, to entertain you and be a good boyfriend. My mom bought me a suit and a rose bouquet. After I skipped the dance and ate at McDonald's alone instead, you told everyone we ditched the dance together and hung out at your place.

We were 16 years old when you kissed me, smelling like garbage. You had a hand on my chest and a drink in the other, and your mouth tasted like Cheetos and Bud-Light. My head went cloudy, as if all my senses were dulled. I couldn't move my arms because they felt cold and heavy, like cement or a rejection. So I stayed still and let you kiss me with your slimy mouth and your groping hand while a rap song about breakups played from someone's phone speaker. Faintly, I heard our friends whooping in the background but they were drowned out by your hiccups and giggles. If anyone asks about it, we both still say it never happened.

I was 17 and you were 18 when I told you I was gay. We were watching soccer practice on the bleachers when you saw Matt Anderson and said you wanted to lick up his jawline. I laughed, took a deep breath, and joked about how he wasn't my type. A breeze passed between us. You chuckled politely but didn't reply, and I hoped it just went over your head. I hoped you hadn't been listening. After lunch that day, you asked him out to dinner and slept with him that night. You texted me to make sure I knew that yeah, he really wasn't my type.

I don't really know how to say anything else. Normally, when I talk to you it's natural and free-flowing. Most nights, my fingers can't move fast enough to type out everything I'm thinking and it feels good if I start crying. We used to stay up until the birds started to chirp, talking about feelings and family and all kinds of teen angst. Today, I've been sitting at my desk typing out the same email for the past 2 hours, and though I feel like I should I haven't shed a single tear. As I write this final email to you, it reminds me of that night when we were 16 and my arms couldn't shove you off no matter how much I wanted them to.

I don't love you. I'll never love you. Your email was touching, and I'll never forget how sincere it was, but I'll also never forget how deceitful and wrong it was either. You talked for paragraphs and paragraphs about how much you love my eyes and the shape of my lips. You recounted every late-night Walmart trip and party in stunning detail, but you left out nights where your hands were on me and you wouldn't let go, you dug your nails in. You left out days where I avoided you, dodged out of your eyesight in the hallways and skipped entire classes just to not talk to you. You seemingly forgot that night you got drunk out of your mind and called me a faggot, begged me to sleep with you, just once, and promised you wouldn't tell anyone. You buried it under "I love you"s and "I miss you"s that only made it worse.

A month ago, I got into the school of my dreams and you got rejected. You assumed I'd follow you to our safety school and I told you I would. But then you went too far, too much, and I panicked alone in my room that night because I couldn't tell anyone what'd happened. I didn't trust anyone else that much except you.

I'm leaving you in this state and running hundreds of miles away from you to a better future at a better school that you could never attend. I'm not answering your messages or your phone calls because I blocked you on every platform. I'm sending you this email because despite everything you've done to me, leaving without a goodbye seems cruel.

So, goodbye.

Why Should She?
Winter Molloy

The snow crunches under a tire.
The morning chill tortures its innocent victims.
Cruel, crazy kids climb onto the boring yellow bus.
They roll their way over the ice,
into the waiting maw of mindlessness.
The girl does not emerge from the house.
Why should she?
Because it's in the rules,
because of the importance of grades,
because of friends.
She does not go, not today.
The life of a hooky is for her.
She will roam the woods with freedom.
She has short brown hair,
and is often mistaken for a boy.
She stands alone in her family's house.
The house is not big,
but the vent is warm.
Who could blame her for choosing warmth?
Her blue eyes stare off into space,
charting the wild unknowns.
She sees that which cannot be seen.
Does she see me?
I believe so.
I think she sees me.
That misfit hooky always wanted to be my mother.

Life's Grey Area
David Lovett

Is it true?
For years it's been: this will look good or this will help
you need to do this and score that
but now, I am living in the moment that all juniors dream of.

Am I done?
No not exactly.
High School is not just based around a place in the future.
It is a place where your future self can look back on and be happy.

So what now?
No I'm not giving up.
Instead, I will break the chains that have bound myself "inside the box"
this time is to solidify friendships and to construct something positive
   to leave behind.

Am I wrong?
I will just say it
no, grades are not the most important part of my school experience now
But I promise, this is a time just as important as any other.

Entrance and Exit

Lucius Atherton

The old rush of adrenaline that used to consume my entire body,
raising my heartrate to an imperishable beat,
filling my blood with a shaking sensation only growing stronger
in the tips of my fingers, transformed into a pure excitement.
I could feel the cold dryness of my hands as I ran them through my hair,
the same hands would have been dripping with sweat only a couple years
    ago.
Just before the entrance my eyes close and I allow the character to enter me.
As my breathing slows to a molasses pace I reach out,
grasping the greatest level of empathy I am capable.
Right when I step into the light I hear my heart racing
as quickly as the beat to a modern dance club song.
I am not at all nervous, now I am awake.
The comfortability and exhilaration hit me hard simultaneously
as if I am being hit by both boiling and freezing water
at the same time but am only spurred on.
Overflowing so I can't help but ignore the overwhelming irony
that I can best understand myself when pretending to be anybody else.
Once I proudly return from the lights, the heat, the approval,
to the dark, cold, abandoned, backstage dugout the high I inhaled on stage
stays with me, stimulating every nerve with a thrilling drug only imitated
    by
my presence on stage.

Alone
Carter Gregg

I adjust the mirrors to the perfect angles,
move my chair to the most comfortable position,
slowly creep backwards,
and then I am off.
My first time I drove alone I felt completely confident of my abilities,
yes, I definitely double checked everything more often than I do now,
but overall, driving went smoothly.
However, something felt off,
I couldn't pin my finger on it right away
    but I knew something was different.
About halfway through my car ride I realized it was the first time
    I had ever been in a car alone. Not driven alone,
but rather been in a car alone.
Before you drive out of your driveway that first time,
you never think how every single time you've been in a car,
it has been with someone.
I always had someone to talk too,
someone to laugh with,
someone to play music for,
but what do I do now?
That's what I remember thinking as I drove alone for the first time.
My mind started darting from thought to thought,
with not a soul to share them with.
Though not at the start,
I grew to love these moments in my car,
I was with my music, my thoughts and nothing else.
Simple as that.

Leaving Home
Michael Babbott

My father and I have a strange relationship. Although we are close, we rarely share deeper feelings or how we might really feel about something. So, when he informed me that our family would be moving to Virginia from Kansas City, I didn't know how to say what I wanted to say. I wrestled with how to tell him that it was crushing me to leave. However, one day, I vividly remember a conversation we had where I just told him everything I was feeling, which was rare for me. I told him about my girlfriend and my best friends, how school was going better, and how I was just learning to love the city. I let out everything I had wanted to say to him, which included some angry, but mostly sad, words. Luckily he just sat and listened, since that was what I really needed. However, what hurt the most was that all my dad could say was "sorry." The future was too uncertain for him to make any promises, so he didn't.

The Photo
Johnson Zhou

My shutterbug mother unwittingly instilled in me from a young age a complicated sentiment about being photographed, as I was always commanded to smile before her camera. Impatient with the ritual, I could not conceal my distaste for what mom considered the "lofty beauty" of life. Posing for pictures became a painful childhood practice. It was not until my fourth journey as a volunteer to an elementary school in Guizhou, China where my grandfather lived and studied, that I overcame my frustration with being photographed.

With rice swaying in the breeze and a little girl named Huiling guiding my way, I meandered along familiar layered terraces, observing the area's unique agricultural style. Over one thousand years ago, my ancestors settled across these towering mountains, growing rices on paddy fields, a system I wanted to modernize for the Dong people.

Lost in thought, I spotted a low, sunlit building at the end of a weed-covered path—the child's home. Huiling ran to the house, her glee undisguised. An old woman wearing a worn but beautiful Dong costume tinkling with small silver bells came to the door. Her humpbacked torso and wrinkles on her forehead told her life stories. She showed obvious confusion upon seeing an unexpected and unfamiliar visitor.

"This is my grandma!" Huiling announced, speaking to her in a dialect I could barely understand. Bursting into a beaming smile and gesturing with sun-leathered hands, the woman said, "Welcome," one of the few words in her dialect I knew.

Carefully surveying the small hut and seeing only the woman and her granddaughter, I learned that she was a "left-behind kid," who only saw her parents one week each year because they left the village to earn better salaries in the city. When the topic moved to her husband, the old woman closed her eyes and lowered her head. Her emotion changed subtly as if she was reminiscing about her remote past. Huiling told me that her grandfather was killed three years previously in a horrific landslide.

I tried to console the woman. "Do you have a picture of him?"

The woman and the girl gazed at each other, sadness in their eyes.

"My grandpa has never had a picture taken, nor did my grandma," Huiling translated. Their emotions were too nuanced for me to understand; was it sorrow or embarrassment?

Standing there, my distaste for my mother's insistent photo sessions evaporated. A heartfelt tenderness awoke, and an unshakable urge beckoned me. "May I take a picture for you, grandma?"

When Huiling translated my message, the old woman's face brightened. Perhaps it was the first time in her life that someone asked to photograph her. Standing proudly, she asked this amateur photographer: "Do I look appropriate for a picture?" Her granddaughter explained her question. I smiled and offered a thumbs-up.

I centered her on my phone screen and asked her to smile. I immediately showed the woman the picture which she eagerly examined. The ambience of the house changed, and she kept nodding and murmuring in delight.

"Grandma really loves her picture," Huiling conveyed her gratitude. Our language barrier dissolved. Pictures had become our common language.

Walking out of the house and bidding my farewell, I felt elated. In taking a picture for the woman, I froze a moment of her family history. We surmounted the obstacles of communication because pictures offered us a precious opportunity to bond and build mutual trust. My desires for the next day surfaced: to print the photo for Huiling's grandmother and to take pictures for another family.

Inspired by the old woman's deep happiness, I realized the value of the family photos on my desk and knew that I would happily comply with my mom's picture-taking obsession thereafter. More importantly, I proudly photographed over fifty families in the village, enabling them to cherish happy moments of their lives in remembering their pasts and those they love.

In Between

Phia Davis

George, no Spencer,
I don't very much like my name.
Family thing
being all noses in the air,
gold embellished plates,
grand pianos in every room.
Honestly I know how to play the ivory ode to elitism
but... well? Nah.
My sister loves it when I play,
if I play,
but I never play.
But, back to the point: I hate my name,
have always gone by Spencer.
It's got that ring to it that
George...
well it just doesn't cut it.
When people hear George
they think kings,
think monkeys,
they think submissive white kids.
Me...
I'm not that,
never have been,
never will be.
My father is mad I've ended up at community college doing liberal arts.
Badly too, might I add.
Honestly school's never been my thing;
business has never been my thing,
and the family business... forget about it.

The stars, philosophy, 80s bands, and poems in a cafe,
that's me.
No, I'm not just some rich kid out to mess
  with daddy's sanity and standards;
everyone thinks that.
I'm just a normal guy
who wants to travel and live a while,
not one for pressed polos
and
black tie dinners.
Ask me something relevant,
Paris or New York?
Paris.
Thailand or Japan?
Thailand.
Colorado or Vermont?
Colorado.
Pastels or pens?
Pastels.
Red roses or daisies?
Both, of course.
Guitars or pianos?
Could one really choose?
The beach or the mountains?
The beach, of course.
I can get lost out there,
pants rolled up,
shoes in my hand,
Maria on my arm,
or is it Marianna?
They come and go so easily,
girls...

They're like the seasons to me,
I can't control the change
or
the moving on.
I have to sit back and watch
as they pass through,
as they take my hand,
then slap it away.
I've learned to stare blankly at that part of my life,
not letting on anything,
not parting the clouds on the thunder and rain inside this lonely heart.
I just fix my hair... a nervous habit,
crack my knuckles,
and stare into the everlasting bouquet of:
Curiosity
Isolation
Discontent
Bliss
That is in fact my life.

18 is < Forever
Claire Longo

Now, I'm no mathematician,
   but I know 18 is less than forever.
Simple math that took me too long to figure out.
As I stand looking out onto adulthood,
I feel hands graze my back, and I brace for the fall.
I was supposed to jump.
To be ready on my own,
   but I wasted my time, and time itself will not wait.
I run to the forever cliff not taking time to breathe,
   but telling myself I can breathe when I get there.

Past tense.
I ran past the age of 14,15,16, and 17 like they were pointless
   busy work given to me by time. I treated 9, 10,11,12, and 13
   as if they were simple mile markers
expressed in inches added to my height, and pounds added on my bones.
Soon everything before 8 became a distant memory, fading further
   and further from view.

Now.
I finally near the cliff and everything familiar is behind me.
It all hits me at once.
Everything I rushed away from can't follow me into the forever.
I am leaving all I had--
being cared for when I was sick,
eating dinner with a family I had called mine since birth,
sleeping in my own bed to wake up to that family I left behind
   the night before,

all the things I tried so hard to escape, yelling, " I'm not a child anymore!"
   with an effortless breath and no regret,
all behind, all far off, and unremembered.
I stop on the edge of the cliff.

I want to turn around. Go back.
Savor it all this time,
   but I feel the hands of time touch my shoulder and spine.
My heart thumps and aches in my chest, radiating toward my head.
I tense.
The math begins to add up.
The obvious was not obvious to me, and what stares me in the face
   is a terrible facade.
18 is less than forever,
and I'm not ready to leave my childhood.
I'm beginning to fall, and I just wish I had done the math.

Arab American
Maryam Alwan

How can you string together a word that is read from left to right
and one that is read from right to left?

That is how I feel.
An eternal tug-of-war, the prelude to a drawing and quartering.
Beckoning to me on each side, the opening and closing of
   my turbulent hyphenation
Arab on one end, American on the other, with me compressed
   in the middle.
and somehow, that short, scaly line connecting the two words
has me feeling anything but.

Embedded like gold flecks in my veins,
the shouted negotiations of shameless vendors on street side markets
and the rich call to prayer,
sweeping strokes of calligraphy morphing into shapes
   that seem to shimmer,
the sickly sweet smell of jasmine
and, for some reason, the lingering, pungent odor of gasoline.

It's as if my parents are fighting over me for custody.
The first is made up of cheek-to-cheek greetings,
fighting over the check in restaurants,
stray cats,
4am breakfasts,
the red-checkered, picnic-cloth headdress my grandfather wears,
and the wooden beads around his neck.

I feel freedom in the clothesline that flies atop a rooftop in Jordan,
overlooking not billboards and flashing lights,
but humble concrete homes,
reaching up to clutch the sky in an embrace.

I hear tranquility within the distinct strums of a oud, a guitar on steroids,
feel at ease at the sight of the Petra desert mountains looming
   in the backdrop,
and see my Middle-Eastern nose on everyone that walks by
   in a crowded mall.

My second custody-seeker is built up of grease stains on a pizza box dying
   to be opened,
the taste of melted cheese on a succulent homegrown burger,
and the scent of a softball turf right after rain,
aching to be clawed up by cleats.

Within the thirteen stripes of our flag are the enticing bright lights
   of New York City,
the syncopation of my palm with my beating heart
as I proudly hear the ringing notes of the National Anthem,
the mouth-watering gravy topping off a hearty Thanksgiving meal,
and, of course, the top-notch education & opportunity
   that can only be found in the home of the brave.

Somewhere in that melting pot, though, I became a little too melted-
My tongue stumbles over Arabic words that should be fluid,
like water droplets pounding against a window,
rather than a rippling, rapid river.

Cut back to me.
In the USA.
The only home I've ever known.
But my own American brothers and sisters are divisive as well.
Tell me, how can I "go back to my own country",
when I was born right here in Thomas Jefferson's hometown?

Remember that tug-of-war I mentioned?
Well, my hands are getting tired and burned,
and the rope is fraying right along with my patience.
Each strand of fiber digging into my skin is a reminder.

Without one side of the hyphen, I wouldn't fit into the other,
and vice versa.
One shoe is too small,
and the other too large.
In order to completely fit in, I need a size in between.

By being forced to choose,
I am being pulled from my roots, each strand being plucked off one by one.
Both of these conflicting cultures are swirled together inside of me,
and if there's one thing I've learned from science,
it's that you can't separate a solid homogeneous mixture.
I should not have to pick a side.

The Quiet Ones

Gabe Yeargan

We all crave something in life
Every single one of us needs something to quell that hunger
   for something more
Sometimes this craving will be food, or some satisfying image or action
Some of us don't ever even find what makes us mad with hunger
But, us quiet ones do.

I'm not talking about those people you see sitting alone in a restaurant
Or even the peaceful type
That find the comfort in a book
I mean the people that you forget exist
The ones you never have talked to
Us quite folk stay hidden
As we do not want to be seen by others
The people that don't want to be social
We find cravings in other activities
If you are one of us and you don't know it
you will probably never find it
And for that I say i'm sorry
If you feel out of place
Uncomfortable in times of intense social interaction
You are probably one of us
You probably have cravings you don't understand
You are probably
A quiet one.

people-watching pt. 2
Mansi Tripathi

a little bell sounds as he pushes through the doors
but he comes in to find the place almost completely empty.
a dozen barren tables stare at him
while he stares back,
unsure of how to make the decision of where to sit down.
it's usually so busy
that he doesn't even have a choice
and,
more often than not,
has to sit at the end of a table
near the overflowing trash can.
he doesn't know how to make this decision.
he doesn't know how to make any decision.
he scans the room
and sees two men chatting excitedly
while sipping their cups of tea.
their hands are completely wrapped around the mugs
to soak up as much warmth as possible.
he's confused.
it's not even cold outside.
he then turns to see two women at a booth
with what,
to them,
must seem like hundreds of books and stray sheets of paper
laid out before them.
he notices that one woman is twirling the pencil in her hand
while her mind wanders
and the other is simply just looking at her.
he doesn't think it looks creepy or weird

but thinks it looks beautiful.
the boy,
who was watching them intently,
had knocked into a table and made a loud noise.
the noise is enough to bring the women back to the present,
and they both smile at each other before returning to their papers.
he hadn't even noticed that they
had been holding hands under the table
and leaving one hand free to work.
he decides that both groups of people
look so happy and content
that he doesn't want to disturb them,
so he finds a small table in the middle and sets down his bag.
he grabs his card from his wallet,
leaving his bag at the table,
and makes his way to the counter.
he asks the woman which one of their drinks
has the most caffeine
and orders two of those.
he barely slept last night.
when he returns to his table,
carrying one drink in each hand
and his card in his mouth,
he sees a woman sitting at his table,
staring at his bag.
he's puzzled by the fact that this woman chose to sit
at a small, already occupied table
while a dozen lay empty
but says hello anyway.
she mumbles but doesn't break her gaze from the book in her hand.
since she's not looking at him,
he takes this opportunity to look at her.

he thinks she looks like the kind of girl
it's easy to make assumptions about,
but promises himself he won't do it.
her face is fully made up
and it's clear that she's been keeping up to date
with recent fashion trends.
she looks well-kept and put together,
and he's intimidated by it.
he then realizes that he actually just made assumptions about her.
he feels bad now.
she pulls out what seem to be very expensive and fancy colored pencils
from her designer bag
and opens the book in her perfectly-manicured hands.
he soon realizes that it's a sketchbook.
she wastes no time.
she starts to draw outlines and shade in the empty white spaces
   on the page.
while coloring,
she grabs one of his drinks and tips it back into her mouth,
leaving lipstick on the rim.
he smiles and doesn't even think that she notices
that it's not hers.
he decides not to say anything
because he doesn't want to disrupt her right now.
he thinks she looks incredible.
moments pass and he tries to do his work on his computer
but still can't stop thinking about the girl sitting right in front of him.
he decides to get up for a second and go to the bathroom,
and,
when he gets back a few minutes later,
sees that the girl is gone.

all that's left on the table is a five dollar bill,
written on with lipstick,
that says, "thanks for the coffee."
he laughs a little and is about to fish his wallet from his bag
when he realizes that something is different.
he pulls a thick white sheet of paper out of his bag and stares at it.
it's the drawing she had been working on.
it's a drawing of him.
he scans the sheet
and turns it over,
looking for any sort of contact information--
an email address,
a phone number,
anything.
but he doesn't find it.
not even a note.
he turns to the other tables to see
that the men are still chatting excitedly
and that the women are still holding hands
and doing their work.
he lays his head on the table
and stares at the colorful drawing before him.

War Zone
Emma Schmidt

I was raised in the middle of a war zone.
Bullets would fly past my head,
bombs exploding all around me.
the hot flames of fire,
would not last they said.

I live walking on eggshells.
They flood every floor inside,
my house that is slowly burning down,
walls crumbling in,
devoured by the hate from outside.

Once I thought the fire stopped,
that the troops had been called back,
and flew away as if they were doves,
that we had laid our weapons down,
oh how wrong I was.

The fire was never put out.
Turns out it was just contained,
but that is not enough to ignore,
everything it took,
and that all it left was pain.

Now I am a war zone.
My head and heart are always in a fight.
I guess it's not surprising,
since war is all I've ever known,
that war has become my life.

Tears of a Murderer
Aimee Straka

when Cain took a stone, jagged, rough like him,
when he watched his once-dear brother
shatter like starlight into a million tiny rays of bone,
and the vermilion soul, red like forbidden fruit,
seep back into the dirt from which man came,
did Cain weep?

even as he stood before a God he knew
could not be fooled, was his body wracked
with the guilt of ending a man's story —
one that had once entwined with his own —
with splatters of bitter vengeance?
was he wracked with the knowledge
that he was alone in this crime?

the one who would have stood behind him
was rotting in a field, flesh no different
than the sheep Abel had raised in life,
now no different than the bleating lamb
that had earned celestial favor
and secured a fate of cold gray murder.

did droplets, not quite holy enough
to cleanse him, stained scarlet, trace their way
down the ruined visage of a man who
could not bear to face such perfect judgement?
the stories say Cain denied, the stories
say anger steeped his syllables, but maybe
they forget his tears, the fear of knowing
that you are the first to steal a soul
and no one can save you.

after all, the Savior taught that we are all
murderers in our ravaging, howling hatred
and so maybe Cain was no different
than any man, except, of course, he wasn't;
there is no mercy for the first.
so perhaps when Cain knelt before the glory
of a God he knew would not forgive,
could not forget,
he wept.

Prelude to Prayer
Marie Ungar

We watched motes of dust drop
through the candlelight
of the church spire & thought
not of falling but flight

finding its resting place
weightlessly. Soft spoken night
bright with heavensweat
acknowledged every exhale.

My breath gravitates outward
when my feet find new ground
until I become more writer,
less thinker, more aria
than chorus. I think truths are better
found than created—

the truth of leaving,
of home, of how we pry
each moment
not for what it has to offer
but for what we won't regret.
Here's the truth: regret

only lives outside the body.
Here's the thought
of what you could be, becoming
a story, voices free of daylight's muzzle
as the streets yield their spines.

Here you are, becoming,
without bells or recital—
just fireflies floating on the notes
of night's descending breath.

Hunger

Baylina Pu

"This is the way the world ends. Not with a bang but a whimper." -T. S. Eliot

Incandescent ache,
famine in the stomach
of the earth. Bleeds
through fault lines,
a low, throaty, slow groan

& not fire/brimstone, no,
but as a body decomposes
beneath the gingko tree,
fingers ginger-root swollen
& knuckle jutting out. Tell the
river the story

of the tiger who drowned,
of sparrows drained along
the current, white neck feathers
a birthmarked noose coiled over
shivering pulse. Mourn only
until the sun sets red, bloated
bread settling into pan.
Yes—history repeats herself
until her voice grows hoarse
and no one is around to listen anymore.

theories of inheritance
Rachel Beling

lamarck said:
it's all carried over in half-memory—
giraffes stretching their necks into oblivion
and the horizon stretching out before you,
longer, longer by the generation.
try to chase the history
of the thoughts you have inherited
and there is no science, no family tree.
there is just graphite from others' words
staining your hands and fingertips until
you see the whorls and become a palm reader.
trace the parasitic lines past primordiality,
and here is your fate.

or you can listen to darwin,
paint cataracts over the old eyes,
maybe keep the veins.
stare at yourself in the mirror,
because you are yourself now.
watch your pupils,
dilating with love or lies,
engulfing you.
instinct will bite through your mind
and maybe blood will seep through your body,
but the words you write are yours—
alone, that strange morse code.
remove your hindsight,
and here is the only place you stand.

and maybe the horizon stretches
just to divide the earth and the sky,
just to remind you what you have stolen
and what you have created.
darwin, lamarck—
you borrowed both.
in your pupils, the lines of your palm.
at the horizon they make—
eyes open, arms outstretched, words not yet spoken—
lamarck said
darwin said
you say

mano po (blessings)
Sarah Mae Dizon

for my nanay

i'm seven in my plaid jumper, my short-sleeved shirt with the smooth,
    rounded collar
long hair thrown over my shoulder, edges rough from a pair of kitchen
    scissors in your careful hands

i'm a curious pair of eyes drinking in the light spilling from the crack in
    the door an ear pressed against the wall and i'm searching for your voice,
    your breath

your face is lost to lamp light, but i catch your pale hands
covering a textbook, tracing the names of all the delicate bones in the
    human body.

short nails, wrinkled knuckles; i'm perched on the counter with swinging
    legs watching your bent fingers clean rice: turning, turning, turning

i like the scrape of grain against bowl, i like the splash of the pouring faucet
    frying fish, the kitchen at dusk, the windows bleed orange on our skin.

i rub my face in your scrubs when you pull me into your arms,
    the cotton is soft and worn down, bright and patterned

the scent of decay and antiseptic sting my nose
and i'm too young to find it anything but comforting;

my hands reach for one of yours: your palm is smooth, a web of creases
    that darken as i curl my fingers into the curl of yours

i press your knuckles against my forehead gentle pressure,
   a passing moment

a message spelled in metacarpals of the words i have yet to learn

or perhaps, may never know

"Mano or Pagmamano is a gesture used in Filipino culture performed as a sign of respect to elders and as a way of accepting a blessing from the elder. Similar to hand-kissing, the person giving the greeting bows towards the offered hand of the elder and presses his or her forehead on the elder's hand." (Wikipedia.)

Anthem
Astrid Weisend

When you set free
the guns and dogs and carnage
and the empty rooms echoed
your name
with cracked lips
on dying breath
I lost my trust in you.

When you sunk back
into yourself and recreated
the torments of our past
on lone stars and
the American dream,
I lost my respect for you.

When you chose
the carnivorous minority
over the desperate majority
that loved you not for
what you had been
but what you could be,
I lost my hope for you.

Until We Let Go
Eliza Sansui

Here's to holding on
to our hearts
for a little longer.
Here's to believing
in someone better
than the boys
fingering our hearts
but refusing to hold them.
Here's to strength in individuality to finding ourselves
futures, hopes, dreams ~our beautiful identities~ before we search
for someone else.
Here's to seeing
the bigger picture
when everyone else
is stuck on a polaroid.
Here's to cozy nights and full hearts wrapped in a blanket
instead of wishing
for someone to hold us.
Here's to waiting for someone
who will love us
and make us love ourselves
love others, and love the world
a little harder.
Here's to thinking with our heads
instead of our hearts
and holding on to our hearts for a little longer.

CVILLE
McKenzie Hall

my city was a marigold,
petals harmonizing in a
honeycrisp breeze,
their edges hazy as if longing
for something bigger
(this was the wrong something bigger)

drench your lips in
saccharine honey and
tell me tales of a time
before this rot settled in
(was there ever a time?)

august 12 2017
red bled into my city
crimson stains of
something bigger
on a backdrop of what once
was golden,
delicate petals
crystallizing in suspense
shattering in shock
(who brought this here
or was it already hiding?)

my city is tinted orange,
yellow folding back over
scarlet scars
left behind by something
that did not belong to us
(we are so much more)

About Our Editors

CROSSROADS VI EDITORIAL STAFF:

Advising Editor **Marie Ungar** is a senior at Albemarle High School and Co-Editor-in-Chief of Sooth Swarm Journal, an online literary/art magazine. When she isn't writing or reading, you can find her listening to good music and craving bubble tea.

Co-editor in Chief **Chloe Whaley** is a junior at Albemarle High School. She has been taking creative writing since seventh grade, and has been a part of the Literary Arts Magazine at AHS for two years. In her free time she enjoys playing volleyball, hiking, and eating food. She also enjoys spending time with her three younger siblings and baking with them.

Co-editor in Chief **Astrid Weisend** is a Junior at Albemarle High School. She is on staff at their literary arts magazine, *the Lantern*, and runs year round. When she has the time to write, she focuses on fiction, particularly science fiction and fantasy.

Managing Editor **Rachel Beling** is a junior at Charlottesville High School, where she is the editor of *Graffiti*, the school's literary magazine. She shares her passion for words with the community by tutoring English as a Second Language students and by providing books through her Little Free Library. Between spells of writing inspiration, she hikes, procrastinates, and ponders the nature of sandwiches.

CONTRIBUTING EDITORS:

Mary Dwyer is a Junior at Albemarle High School. She has worked on her school's literary magazine and was over the moon to be able to help create this anthology. She has been published multiple times (her first time being the fourth edition of this anthology) and hopes to continue writing though college and into her adult life.

Artina Li is a tenth grader at Albemarle High School. She loves to writing poetry and prose, listening to music, and watching anime. From working with the crossroads anthology she learned to appreciate more writing styles, and new perspectives to view works for publishing. Lost in thought and a blurry future beyond, she is learning to tone down her cynicism and stay more positive.

Baylina Pu is a junior at Albemarle High School and the literature editor of her school's literary-art magazine. She is the holder of numerous awards such as from the Scholastic Art & Writing Awards and the Virginia High School League, among others. In addition to writing, Baylina enjoys creating art, playing music, performing, and making puns.

Phia Davis is a high school aged college student pursuing her associates in Liberal Arts at PVCC. She wrote with the Monticello High School newspaper, The Hoofprint. Currently she is part of the editorial staff for the Tupelo Press Teen Writing Center. Phia has enjoyed working on this year's Crossroads VI anthology, and organize the weekly teen writing meetings. She has loved creative writing since she can remember and enjoys spending her time writing.

Winter Sky Molloy is a homeschooler/dual enrollment student at Piedmont Virginia Community College, but that is not what she is. If she must be defined she should be defined by the dozens of stories, characters, and fantastic realms that populate her mind. There is rarely a time when some sort of story is not sorting itself out at the front of her brain. She also draws manga stories, makes copper jewelry, and is writing a fantasy novel.

Laurel Molloy is a writer, a nature lover, a soccer player. Writing has taught her who she wants to be, and what she wants to believe. She finds that imagination and thought are a form of reality just as much as, what she sees, hears, and feels.

Participating students came from the follow area high schools:

Albemarle High School
Monticello High School
Western Albemarle High School
Charlottesville High School
The Miller School
St. Anne's Belfield
The Renaissance School

www.ingramcontent.com/pod-product-compliance
Lightning Source LLC
Chambersburg PA
CBHW032045290426
44110CB00012B/954